CORPORATE CREDIT UNLEASHED

EVERYTHING YOU BETTER KNOW ABOUT BUILDING CORPORATE CREDIT WHEN YOUR PERSONAL CREDIT SUCKS

KEVYN J. NELSON

www.worldwidecreditandfinancialsolutionsinc.com

DISCLAIMER

Worldwide Credit and Financial Solutions, Inc cannot be responsible for errors in the preparation of the materials, nor the presentation of the same. We expressly limit our damages to the amount that you paid for this manual. You are advised that this manual is presented to stimulate learning. For specific advice, prior to taking any action, consult with the expert, attorney, accountant, etc., of your selection.

This manual is a guide for educational purposes only.
Worldwide Credit and Financial Solutions, Inc is not offering advice, legal or other, in any fashion. Every vendor has its own credit policies and they are subject to change at any time.

Introduction

Stop using your personal credit to establish credit for your business! This manual serves as a tool in helping businesses, churches and ministries obtain business credit without using their personal credit. The types of businesses we have assisted are:

Lawn Care Service

Daycares

Restaurants

Churches (large and small)

Hair Salons

Barber Shops

Trucking Companies

Pressure Washing

Music Studios

Home-Based Businesses

Dance Studios

Non- Profits

Entertainment Companies

And many more...............

Many vendors will check your business credit report before making critical decisions about your business. With our solid knowledge and years of experience, the business credit building tools used in this manual have helped businesses establish business credit without using one's own personal credit.

Worldwide Credit and Financial Solutions Inc will show you how business credit can help your company obtain:

- Major credit cards

- Office supply accounts

- Equipment leases

- Store credit cards

- Lines of credit

In this manual, WWCFS Inc uses solid business principles essential in getting a new credit report for every business you start. Having good business credit will be simple once you master the principles in our guide, even if you have poor personal credit! Additional benefits with our guide are:

- How to set up your business.

- The different business structures in creating a business.

Our formula will help separate and protect your personal assets from your company's assets by establishing a full credit profile. At that point you will join the world's largest business database with over 100 million businesses and growing! Why not get better interest rates and credit terms from banks and lenders? This manual you easy, step-by-step instruction that outlines how easy it is to establish corporate credit without the assistance of professionals who charge thousands of dollars! Congratulations on taking the first steps as an entrepreneur in doing business smarter! We at Worldwide Credit and Financial Solutions Inc wish you the very best in achieving your business dream.

Table of Contents

What is Business Credit?

B
usiness credit is the single largest source of business financing by volume, even exceeding bank loans (Source: National Association of Credit Management). Business credit is different from consumer credit, angel investor financing, and venture capital financing. Why? Because business credit is the credit extended between businesses, usually for the purpose of acquiring equipment, goods or services that will eventually be resold or used to generate a profit.

How do you get Credit?

As a customer, being granted business credit is a privilege by the creditor to defer the payment of a debt over time. Like consumer credit grantors (e.g., credit card companies), business credit grantors evaluate the creditworthiness of the credit applicant to determine whether or not to issue credit. That evaluation is based heavily on the applicant's business credit score.

Establishing credit for a business is a process that should be done over time. The older the business the more options the business will have to build credit without the use of personal guarantees. It's not as hard as one would think. The first step is to start building business credit now.

<u>*Who are the Business Credit Bureaus?*</u>

There are two major business credit-reporting agencies in the United States: Dun & Bradstreet and
Experian:
- Dun & Bradstreet at www.dnb.com
- Experian Business Credit Services at www.experian.com

Most of the creditors utilize information provided through Dun & Bradstreet to create their credit information reports. Though many different companies collect and disseminate credit information on businesses in America, Dun & Bradstreet and Experian are the credit-reporting bureaus that most companies use.

Dun & Bradstreet

Dun & Bradstreet is the largest business credit-reporting bureau with over 75% of the business credit reporting market. The website offers user-friendly tools for the business owner to check for their business listing and the feedback from the clients and customers. Dun & Bradstreet allows you to establish the framework for your business credit profile for $499. However, if you are not pressed for time and don't need your credit scores right away, there is another way to do this for $0. We will explain how in the next few pages. Dun & Bradstreet offers a free Dun & Bradstreet number. This option does not establish a business credit profile. If you opt not to pay for any of their products and services the process takes about 4-6 weeks to receive your business Dun &Bradstreet number. On the pages that follow, we will show you how to build your profile and get your Duns number in 48 hours, absolutely free. Isn't that amazing?

Experian

Experian manages large databases on consumers and businesses, but when it comes to business credit reporting, Experian's scoring system, known as Scorex Plus, is not as often used by credit grantors as the Dun & Bradstreet Paydex scoring system.

6

What Is a Paydex Score?

A Paydex score is similar to a FICO score, only it determines your business credit worthiness. In comparison, having a 75 Paydex score is like having a FICO score of 750. It is not uncommon for a business to be listed with Dun & Bradstreet and not know it. To find out if your business is listed please visit http://www.dnb.com/. Your company may already have a Paydex score and you may not even know it.

Steps to take to view your credit report for free

1. Go to www.dnb.com

2. Look near the bottom on the left side and click on "Update Your Credit Profile Online."

3. Click "Sign up now" on the next page.

4. If you don't know your Dun & Bradstreet number put in your company name and address.

5. Enter your information in the form exactly as you have set up your business. Make sure that the phone number that you use for your business is the same. Also, if you are not incorporated yet or an LLC under "Title" click "Owner."

6. Once the form is complete you will either get an email with your e-update password and Duns number.

7. If you get an email stating that the information did not match, give D&B a call to update your businesses information.

Business Credit Rating

Will Having a Business Credit Rating help me with a Loan?

The best analogy is to think of your corporate credit to that of a house. First, build a solid foundation, and then you can build the house. This philosophy is the same for building corporate credit; it is a time-based accomplishment. The common mistake among business owners is thinking a good business credit score will qualify the corporation for a bank loan. A good corporate credit score is only one piece of what is needed. The credit score is only one of the items a bank might look at to make its decision.

Just because your corporation has a 75-80 Paydex score does not demonstrate the corporation's "financial ability" to repay a loan. Furthermore, building business credit does not eliminate all the information a bank would need to give a business loan.

☐ Bank financing
☐ Loans
☐ Equipment leasing

Large ticket items will usually require the corporation to produce financials or a personal guarantor to show evidence that the corporation can repay the loan. If your corporation has the cash flow and profit, then certainly bank loans, equipment loans, and real estate deals are achievable without using personal credit. However, if the corporation is two months old and has just achieved a great business credit score, the score alone would not qualify your company for a loan. The items listed above will likely be required.

While your company is still in the early stages of obtaining business credit from companies, you must have realistic expectations because earning credit to obtain leases and purchase tangible items such as open lines of credit with companies that provide products and services is a process that does not happen overnight. Just because you may have a personal credit score of 750 does not necessarily qualify you to purchase a $950,000 home. You must have the financial ability to repay the loan as well.

8

Why Business Owners Shouldn't Use Their Personal Guarantee to Obtain Business Credit

There are a few reasons business owners should not use their personal guarantee on business credit. First, the individual signer is liable if the business cannot make the payments as agreed. Second, they risk the chance of lowering their own personal credit scores, negatively affecting the individual's personal debt to ratio income, and much more.

Obtaining credit for a business is a process that should be established over time. The older the business the more options the business will have to build credit and obtain loans and leases without the use of personal guarantees. Even though the process seems lengthy and time consuming it is well worth the wait.

How and Why You Should Build a Business Credit Profile

Using personal savings in the beginning of financing most small businesses, or assets of the owners can rapidly reach a stage of growth where they are forced to seek credit or investment solutions to fund that growth. On the other hand, I am going to teach you how to build your business credit profile in order to assist you in obtaining the financing you need to grow and succeed. As a business owner, ask yourself the following questions listed below:

- Are you looking for a business loan or financing?
- Have you been turned down?
- Do you need a business line of credit for working capital or growth?
- Do you want to lease or finance equipment for your business?

As a business owner the most vital part in the growth of a small business is funding. Not only is it important to have the right funding in place, but it is also the most important factor in having a strong foundation of your small business. Business owners quickly understand that applying for business funding is a much more difficult process than applying for personal credit. Applying for business funding requires preparation. You must understand the building process and what it takes to qualify.

When you apply for business funding such as a bank loan, funding sources will likely look at your personal credit and the business credit profile to determine: If they will approve your request; the amount; and if you will have to give a personal guarantee. The chart on the next page illustrates the incredible amount of savings by having a "favorable business credit profile."

Let's say you have a personal credit FICO score of 660, but no business credit. Based upon your personal credit, you are granted a business loan of $100,000 on terms of 13% interest over 10 years. If there had been a favorable business credit profile, the terms on the same loan might have been 7% interest over 10 years resulting in the savings of thousands of dollars.

No matter what your financing needs are, it is possible to secure funding for your business. Good or bad credit, it's a matter of getting the capital you're looking for and knowing where to go. Knowing how to successfully build your business credit profile is the key to success.

When Should You Build Your Business Credit Profile?

One of the keys to building business credit is knowing where you stand right now. Do you? You must know what every funding source is going to look at before you apply. If you don't you are completely wasting your time and will most likely be declined. In other words, "Pre-Qualify Your Business." There are over 5,000 institutional sources for obtaining business capital in the United States and each one has different criteria. Each one will tell you NO for just "1" thing.

Less than 3% of businesses that attempt to receive funding on their own ever do! If you apply at multiple places without pre-qualifying your business, you risk the chance of damaging your credit and will eliminate your chances of receiving approvals from just the source that would have approved your application. It is a good idea to start building business credit at least 3-6 months before your business will need funding. Start by doing a Business Credit Assessment on you and your business.

Business Credit Assessment

1. What steps have you taken to build your business credit?

_____

2. Can I stand to improve my personal credit?

_____

3. What is my available credit?

_____

4. How old is my business?

_____

5. Do I have any trade references?

_____

6. How much business credit do I need?

_____

7. How will I use business credit?

_____

8. How would business credit help my business?

_____

11

The Business Credit Building Process

Step I: *Formalize the Business and Choose a Business Structure*

Regardless of how you choose to operate your business, in order to build a business credit profile you must have a "formal" structure. There are five different types of business structures in forming a company:

> Sole Proprietor
>
> C-Corporation
>
> L.L.C. Limited Liability Company
>
> L.L.P. Limited Liability Partnership
>
> S-Corporation

It is very important to know what type of company you are forming in regards to how much personal liability one has in operating a business. It's best to weigh the pros and cons in business operating alternatives.

Sole Proprietorship

Easy to start; owner and business are one in the same; owner is exposed to liability for business debts; if owner conducts business under a trade name, a DBA or "Doing Business As" must be filed with the cities or county.

C-Corporation

Owners are called stock or shareholders; ownership is easily transferable; owners are taxed at the corporate and shareholder levels (double taxation); corporation is a separate entity from owners; shareholders are not personally liable for business debts; requires filing of Articles of Incorporation with the Secretary of State. S-Corporation Limited ownership; no double taxation; income or loss is passed through to the owners; requires filing of Articles of Incorporation with the Secretary of State and IRS form SS-4 (S-Election).

12

Limited Liability Corporation (L.L.C.)

Limited personal liability of owners; unlimited number of owners; owners pay taxes based on their share of ownership; requires filing of Articles of Organization with the Secretary of State.

Limited Liability Partnership (L.L.P.)

Similar to the L.L.C., but designed for professional organizations such as CPAs and attorneys; requires filing of Articles of Organization with the Secretary of State Limited Partnership. Consists of at least one general partner and other limited partner or general partner is personally liable for the partnership's debts; limited partners are not personally liable, as long as they do not materially participate in the partnership's management; partners are taxed based on ownership percentages; requires filing a Partnership Registration with the Secretary of State. Once you have chosen how you will operate, you need to file your Articles of Incorporation, Articles of Organization, Partnership Agreement or "Doing Business As" with your Secretary of State or your respective Secretary of State. The cost to file will vary by state.

S-Corporation

An S-Corporation is a corporation for all purposes except for taxes. For tax purposes it is treated very similarly to a partnership. This means that S-Corporations don't pay income tax but report the results of their operations to the shareholders who report their share of corporate income or loss on their personal taxes.

Step II: Filing the pertinent paperwork

Obtain a Federal Tax ID Number

Applying for your Tax Id (EIN #) is really simple. By going to www.irs.gov and clicking on the link that says "Business" at the top of the page and from there click on "Employer ID Number" and you can have your new tax ID number in about 5 minutes. Be sure to not put in any punctuation marks or special characters or your request will not go through.

Business License

Every business is required to have a business license in order to operate. Be sure to check with your local city hall to find out the steps that need to be taken in order to obtain a business license.

Open a Bank Account in the name of the business

A business bank account reference is a must have in the building business credit process. Creditors believe that if you have opened up a business bank account that you have taken your business seriously and it is not just a hobby. Opening a bank account should not be a hard thing to do. Some business owners have had some unfortunate events to take place and that caused them to be put in Check Systems or Tele Check. Don't fret! There are many banks out that do not run your personal information through those systems as long as you are a corporation or LLC. Be sure to do your research before you apply. Please note that most banking institutions require an EIN, business license, and incorporation status before opening an account.

Set-Up a Commercial Office

Regardless if you are a home-based business the important thing is to not look like a home-based business on paper. Below are a few options to help you reach that goal:

- Having your business telephone number listed with 411 is a must!
- Having an office address in a commercial location.

Establishing your business as a "commercial" business instead of a home-based business lets credit grantors know that your business is a viable one — they will also be able to verify your business status by checking with the telephone company and validating the address you gave is zoned for a business. Below you will find another alternative to forming your commercial location.

Virtual Offices - Shared office space for small businesses usually operated by local office buildings. Below you will find a few recommendations:

- HQ GlobalWorkplaceshttp://www.hq.com
- Office Suites PLUS http://officesuitesplus.com

*******WARNING*******

Please don't use a mailbox store or P.O. Box as the
physical address of your business. However, they can be used as your
company's billing address and is some cases a shipping address.*

Virtual business line

What is a virtual number? "It's a telephone number outside of the physical area code you reside in and it's provided by telephone carriers and VoIP providers". It allows callers to make local calls from that area code to your phone. For example, if you live in Atlanta and have a virtual phone number with a San Francisco area code, anyone calling from San Francisco is making a local call. There are many companies that offer virtual numbers with the area code that you may live in or toll-free numbers.

Ureach.com, Ringcentral.com, Onebox.com, Vonage.com, and Earthlink.com are just a few to choose from. Be sure to do an internet search for the best virtual number for your company. If you decide to obtain a virtual number you can go to www.listyourself.net, www.yellowpages.com to list your phone number in the 411 data base. This option will keep you from having to pay for a phone line to be installed in your home if you are running a home-based business. *Warning: not all carriers will list*

Virtual Fax Numbers

Every company must have a separate fax number from their business phone line. A virtual fax number works great because there are no extra phone lines to install. With a virtual fax you are issued a fax number that goes directly to your email account. Once you receive your fax via email you print it out and that's it! If it is a fax that needs to be signed, then you will need a fax machine to return the fax. You can always go to your local office supply store to return a fax. We suggest that you eventually purchase a fax machine. Efax.com and Packetel.com are great companies to establish fax numbers and send email to fax functions at a low monthly cost.

www.efax.com
wwwpacketel.com

Step 3: Setting up the Business Credit Profile

Obtaining a DUNS Number

Dun & Bradstreet is the company that tracks your business. Every business needs a DUNS number which is your business social security number. You can apply for a DUNS number on the Dun & Bradstreet website. If you do not plan on paying the $499 it can take up to 30- 45 days to obtain your Dun and Bradstreet number.

Now, if your company plans on applying for a government grant then you can receive your Dun and Bradstreet number in 48 hours. Apply for your D&B number at www.dnb.com.

Steps to getting DUNS # in 48 hours

1. Go to http://www.ccr.gov/

2. Click on "Find my DUNS" on the left side.

3. Follow the prompts and register.

4. You must know your companies SIC Code in order to complete this process

www.osha.gov/oshstats/sicser.html

16

Tips on Applying for a DUNS Number

NEVER supply your financial information. Why? Dun & Bradstreet is in the business of making money and any information that you supply to them they will sale to any of your competitors if they pay for it. For instance, you report one year because your company had a great year and the following year your company had record losses? Would you want your competitors to know that?

Unless your company has revenue of $1 million or more I suggest that you not report your finances, but the decision is yours. In order to help establish your business for longevity purposes, it is best to state that your business is at least 4-5 years old. It benefits your business profile. Keep in mind that even if you've only recently incorporated the business, it's possible that you've been operating as a sole proprietorship prior to that point. In other words, it's a common occurrence to have a recent incorporation of a 4-5 year old business.

Additionally, your employee status should be at least 10-25 and upward of 50 employees instead of a one or two person establishment because it may not be viewed as being a stable enough company for some creditors. And, unlike personal credit, with business credit the higher credit ratings are reserved for the largest companies.

Step 4: *Applying for Business Credit*

How to Apply for Credit

The reasons businesses can't find funding are:

- Not knowing where to look for the "right" funding source.

- Not knowing how to pre-qualify before they apply.

- Not knowing how to successfully present their request.

- They're missing "just one thing" and they will hear NO.

- They don't know how "shooting blindly" will kill their chances.

"Shooting Blindly" is sending your deal to multiple lenders at the same time without pre qualifying before you apply. Some lenders say "NO" because they don't do the type of funding you want or your deal doesn't meet their exact funding criteria. The rest say "NO", even though they would have done your deal, because no lender wants to be third, fourth, or fifth in line. Remember, creditors can be lazy.

Example: if your company name is ABC & D Inc and a creditor does a search for your business and they enter ABC and D and nothing comes up then they will deny you on the spot. Prior to starting my own business I worked in the credit department for a major corporation.

Now speaking from experience I know that creditors do what they want to do. I've witnessed creditors pull a credit report on a company and some days they wouldn't bother. Some days they would go by company policy and some days they would give companies a chance to prove themselves. With that said, you can never be 100% sure of a creditors criteria.

18

How to successfully apply for business credit:

- Know every funding source's exact criteria for providing funding.
- Have a system that allows you to pre-qualify before you apply.
- Have an accounts payable person.
- Know how much revenue your company makes or plans to make.
- Know the credit terms of the credit grantor.

Creditors will ask how much revenue your company generates. As a new company, you have not generated any revenue. Review your business plan or have strategic goals of your revenue for the upcoming year to get past that obstacle. The goal is to make your company look as stable as possible. For example, Jane Doe should not be the President and the Accounts Payable person.

(A/P)Accounts Payable means the person responsible for handling the bills for your company. If you plan on having a partner we suggest that you use his/her name as that A/P person. Listed below are key terms regarding "net terms" and "revolving accounts"

Terms:

Net Terms: Payments are applied to specific invoices. A monthly statement (with invoices attached) with balance normally due within 30 days after the statement date. Read your invoice carefully because some companies may be net 10, 15 or 20

Revolving Account: Payments are applied to the total balance, not specific invoices. One can pay his/her balance in full when due, or, to help manage cash flow, make minimum monthly payments with finance charges.

Now that you have taken the steps to establish your business the correct way it is time to start applying for credit. Due to the newness of your company there are certain credit accounts that your company will not qualify for right out of the gate.

The key is to obtain a Paydex score without having to pay the $499 to Dun and Bradstreet to get it. In order to get a Paydex score you must have at least 5 vendors report your payment history on your Dun and Bradstreet report.

There are certain vendors that will extend your company credit and report that you paid them on time without you having to pay Dun and Bradstreet to report them.

Now if you don't want to wait the 3-8 months to get your Paydex score and you HAVE creditors other than the ones listed in this manual then you can pay the $499 fee to D&B and get your score a lot sooner. The vendors that are listed below automatically report to D&B without you having to pay. Because some of the vendors listed below have contracts to auto report to D&B if you tried to pay the $499 to have them added quicker D&B will not accept them.

Time to Build Credit!

Below is a list of companies that will extend business credit. Apply immediately after your business has been established correctly. These companies can help you get the Paydex score that your company needs to open up greater doors. Please remember that patience is a virtue in establishing business credit. There are companies that will extend credit without having a Paydex score.

If the application suggests a Dun and Bradstreet number and you don't have a Paydex score yet, I would suggest that you not apply until you get it. In order to open an account, some of the companies below will require you to purchase merchandise prior to opening a new account. Stay under $100 and the account will be opened without prepayment. In certain instances a vendor may require that you pre pay your order. If this happens it is best to go ahead and pre pay so that the account can be opened so your payment history can be reported.

Our Suggestion*

- Reliable www.reliable.com (Make a purchase online or call and request a catalog)
- Nebs www.nebs.com (Make a purchase online)
- Staples www.staples.com (Make sure that you have gotten your Dun & Bradstreet number and that your company is showing in their system. Go to dnb.com to do a search for your company)
- Uline-www.uline.com
- Rapidforms- www.rapidforms.com
- Quill- www.quill.com (They may require that you submit a credit application if they cannot locate your business in the D&B system

A good rule of thumb is to pay your invoice at least a week before they are due. Why? Because you want your creditors to report your on time payment history. If you need more supplies, it will be acceptable to place another order. The more orders that you place, the more credit you are building. Once you have established your Paydex score of 75 or above, the key is keeping it! The only way to keep your score good is to pay all bills on time and make sure that you order from your 2 or more of your suppliers monthly.

*Requirements are subject to change

What's next?

Once you have received your Paydex score you can now apply to the companies listed below. Now was that hard? You now know the steps to building business credit. Worldwide Credit and Financial Solutions Inc wishes you continued success.

- Home Depot - www.homedepot.com/cards

- Amazon.com - www.amazon.com

- American Needle – www.americanneedle.com (clothing)

- Arco – www.arco.com

- Barnes & Noble - www.barnesandnoble.com (apply under Purchase order account)

- Best Buy - www.bestbuy.com - www.bestbuybusiness.com

- Borders – www.borders.com Citgo Fleet - www.citgo.com

- BP Master Card – www.bp.com

- Chevron/Texaco –www.chevron.com

- Citi Business Cards – www.citibusinesscreditcards.com

- Conoco / Phillips 66 / 76 - www.conoco.com

- Dell Computers - www.dell.com

- Deluxe – www.deluxe.com

- Exxon/Mobile- www.exxon.com

- FedEx / Kinkos - www.fedexkinkos.com

- Gemplers- www.gemplers.com

- HD Expo - www.expo.com

- Home Depot Master Card - www.homedepot.com/cards

- Lowes Commercial - www.lowes.com

- Marathon – www.marathon.com

- Nextel - www.nextel.com

- Northern Tools - www.northerntool.com

- Office Depot - www.officedepot.com

- Office Max - www.officemax.com
- Pens – www.pens.com
- Quill.com - www.quill.com
- Perazzi Apparel – www.Perazziapparel.com
- Radio Shack - www.radioshack.com
- Sam's Club – www.samsclub.com
- Savannah Suites – www.savannahsuites.com
- Sears- www.sears.com
- Shell Fleet - www.shell.com
- Sprint –www.sprint.com
- Sunoco Corporate - www.sunoco.com
- Rapid Forms- www.rapidforms.com
- Rapid Fuel - www.rapidfuel.com
- T-mobile - www.tmobile.com
- Target –www.target.com
- TigerDirect - www.tigerdirect.com
- Toys R Us – www2.toysrus.com/guest/corpsales.cfm
- UPS – www.ups.com
- Valero –www.valero.com
- Wright Express - www.wrightexpress.com

Other Resources

Internet Sources

1800-flowers.com
http://ww2.1800flowers.com/flowers/corporate/benefits.asp

3M Company
http://solutions.3m.com/wps/portal/!ut...VAQA-irWmQ!!

AAMCO Transmissions
http://www.aamcotransmissions.com/na...g_options.html

AAMCO Transmissions
http://www.aamcotransmissions.com/national...ng_options.html

Air Culnaire (Food Service)
http://www.airculinaire.com/ordering.asp

Alson's Jewelry
http://www.alsonjewelers.com/services.htm

Amherst Technologies
http://www.amherst1.com/

Amtech
http://www.amtechdisc.com/payment.htm

ASAP Coach (Limousine Company)
http://www.asapcoach.com/openAccount.htm

AT&T (Phone Services)
www.att.com

A-Vidd Electronics
http://www.a-vidd.com/pdf/aviddcreditapp.pdf

Axion Tech
http://www.axiontech.com/corp.php

Bacario
http://www.bacario.com/Corporate.asp

Ballantye Resort (Hotel)

24

http://www.ballantyneresort.com/

Bed, Bath & Beyond
http://www.bedbathandbeyond.com/CorpSales.asp?order_num=-1

Belize Bank (Visa Corporate Credit Account) (NO PG REQUIRED)
http://www.belizebank.com/pdfs/CorporateCr...Application.pdf

Billing Direct (affiliate program, like CJ.com)
http://www.billingdirect.net/

BladeSmart
http://bladesmart.com/bladesmart.com/statp.../corpsales.html

Bloomingdale's
http://www1.bloomingdales.com/about/shopping/corporate.jsp#

Boston Coach (Limousine Company)
http://www.bostoncoach.com/common/resources/account.jsp

Bridgestreet (Corporate Housing)
www.bridgestreet.com

Carey International (Limousine Company)
www.careyint.com

Circuit City Business Sales
http://business.circuitcity.com/b2b_landing_page.htm

Cognigen PCs
https://www.cognigen-pc.com/main/eaccount/c...pplication.aspx

Continental Airlines
http://www.continental.com/programs/uatp/

Corporate Express
http://www.corporateexpress.com/faq.html

Corporate Outfitter
http://corporateoutfitter.cabelas.com/

Crestwood Suites (Hotel)
http://www.crestwoodsuites.com/cwdirbill.p...0Bill%20Account

Davel (Limousine Company)
www.davel.com

Discount Awards
http://www.discountawards.com/CorpAccounts.asp

Disney
http://disneymeetings.disney.go.com/dwm/in...oupOverviewPage

DTV City
http://www.dtvcity.com/help/corporate.html

Earthlink Business Services
http://www.earthlink.net/biz/majoraccounts/

EBC Computers
http://www.ebccomputers.com/Documents/netterms.PDF

Empire Limousine (Limousine Company)
www.empireint.com

Exclusive Tickets
http://www.exclusivetickets.com/corporateInfo.cfm

Fairytale Brownies
http://www.brownies.com/Corporate%20Credit%20Application.doc

Franklin Sports
http://www.franklinsports.com/fsm/files/cr...application.pdf

FTD.com
http://www.ftd.com/528/corporate/

GAP
http://www.gapincbusinessdirect.com/index.asp

Gempler's
http://www.gemplers.com/a/pages/corpsales.asp

GETTY GAS
http://www.getty.com/gettycardapp.pdf#

Greyhound Bus
www.greyhound.com

Handago
http://www.handango.com/Information.jsp?si...CKey=1_BUSINESS

Harley Davidson
http://www.harley-davidson.com/wcm/Content/Pages/HDFS/financial_services.jsp?locale=en_US

Headsets
http://www.headsets.com/headsets/credit/cr...pplication.html

Hertz
http://www.hertztrucks.com/business/bap.pdf

Hewitt Packard HP
www.hp.com

Hilton Hotels
www.hilton.com

Huntington Bank (Relocation Direct Bill Service)
http://www.huntington.com/pas/HNB1725.htm

Hyatt Regency Lake Tahoe
http://www.cflr.com/courses/Dir_billing.pdf

HydePark Jewelers
http://www.hydeparkjewelers.com/HPSite/dep...application.pdf

IBM Computers
www.ibm.com

Ideal Industries
http://www.idealindustries.com/pdf/EndUserSetUpForm.pdf

Ingram Micro
http://www.ingrammicro.com/

Jacopos (Pizzeria)
http://www.jacopos.com/CorporateAccounts.htm

JDR Micro Computers
www.jdr.com/premier

JEB Leasing Company
http://www.jebleasing.com/apply.html

Kohls
http://www.kohlscorporation.com/GiftCard/GiftCards01.htm

Korman Communities (Corporate Housing)
www.korman1.com

L.L. Bean
http://www.llbean.com/corporateSales/?feat=ln

Linens n Things

http://www.lnt.com/corp/index.jsp?page=cor...2_corpsales_txt

Luberman's building
http://www.lumbermens-building.com/pdf/con...-credit-app.pdf

Luggage Pros
http://www.luggagepros.com/

Macys
http://www1.macys.com/store/corporate/index.jsp?bhcp=1

Masters Inn (Hotels)
www.mastersinn.com

Metro Hosting (Web Hosting Provider)
http://www.hostingmetro.com/

Mitsubishi Digital Electronics America
http://www.mitsubishi-tv.com/

Monster (They give net 14 terms)
www.monster.com

Monte Vista
http://www.mvcoop.com/credit/index.asp

My Coffee Supply
http://www.mycoffeesupply.com/corp_login.asp

My Tool Store
www.mytoolstore.com

Northwest Builder's Network Inc
http://www.nwbuildnet.com/help/credit.html

Oakwood (Corporate Housing)
www.oakwood.com

Patagonia
http://www.patagonia.com/custserv/corporate_sales.shtml

Peapod Food Delivery Service
www.peapod.com

Pioneer Electronics (USA) Inc.
http://www.pioneerelectronics.com/pna/cont...l?fpSiteId=2076

Powell Company

www.powellcompany.com

REI
http://www.rei.com/cgs/?stat=footer_corp_sales

Rio Pavilion (Hotel)
http://www.harrahs.com/our_casinos/rlv/gro...ll_app_form.pdf

Rose City Software
http://www.rosecitysoftware.com/corporate/

Saab
http://www.saabfleet.com/

Sam's Club Credit Account
http://www.onlinecreditcenter2.com/sams/rf...app_direct.html

Samys
http://www.samys.com/industrial.php?PHPSES...8f5165a2082651f

Savoya (Limousine Company)
www.savoya.com

SelectATicket.com
http://www.selectaticket.com/CorporateAccounts.asp

Sencore
http://www.sencore.com/orderinfo/corpopen.htm

Sharper Image
http://www.sharperimage.com/corporatesales/

Sonesta Hotel and Suites
http://www.sonesta.com/coconut_grove/page.asp?pageID=10904

Staceys
http://www.staceys.com/corporatesales.html

Starbucks
http://www.starbucks.com/business/bizgifts.asp

Super Shuttle (Limousine Company)
https://www.supershuttle.com/webrez/Update.aspx

Surray Luggage
http://www.surrayluggage.com/corporatesales.html

Thrifty
http://www.thrifty.com/images/rx/img2076.pdf

Toys R Us
http://www2toysrus.com/guest/corpSales.cfm.

TradeName.com
https://www.tradename.com/fees/corpacc.html

United States Postal Service
www.usps.com

US LUGGAGE
http://www.usluggage.com/corpsales.htm

USA LEGAL FORMS
http://www.uslegalforms.com/accountopen.doc

Vac Hut Plus, Inc.
http://www.vachutplus.com/corpacct.htm

Viracon
http://www.viracon.com/corporateCreditApp.html

Waiter.com (food take out company)
http://www.waiter.com/documents/waiter-corp-account-form.pdf

Walgreens
http://www.walgreens.com/about/community/g...rds/default.jsp

Weems Plath
http://www.weems-plath.com/corporate_sales.html

Wilkinson's Flowers
http://www.wilkinsonsflowers.com/help.asp

Williams-Sonoma
www.williams-sonomainc.com/bsa/index.cfm

Other Resources, Phone Contacts

- Best Buy - Status; 1 (800) 811-7276

- Borders (734) 477-1039 - Fax Application: 1 (877) 254-9229 - Status Update

- BP/Amoco Status Update: 1 (800)365-6204

- Chevron/Texaco Business Card Status Update: 1 (888) 243-8358

- Citgo Fleet; (734) 477-1039 - Fax Application: 1 (877) 254-9229 - Status Update

- Citi AA: 1 (888) 662-7759

- Citibank Status: 1 (800) 645-7240, 1 (800) 288-4653, 1 (800) 750-7453

- Conoco - Status Line, automated 1 (866) 289-5622

- Experian Business: 1 (888) 211-0728

- Exxon Mobil Business Card: 1 (800) 903-9966

- HD Commercial: 1 (800) 685-6691

- HDMC Sondee: 1 (877) 969-9030

- Home Depot MC 1 (877) 969-9039

- Key Bank: 1 (800) 254-2737

- Liz Claiborne: (212)354-4900

- Lowe's - Status; 1 (800) 445-6937

- Lowe's – Underwriter: 1 (866) 232-7443

- Lowe's Fraud/UW: 1 (800) 444-1408

- MBNA – 1 (800) 673-1044

- Meijers MC: (801) 517-5560

- Office Depot - Status Line, automated 1 (800) 767-1358

- Office Depot; 1 (800) 767-1358, 1 (800) 729-7744 automated line to check

- Office Max - Status Line, automated: 1 (800) 283-7674

- OFFICEMAX STATUS: 1 (800) 283-7674

- Philips 66: 1 (866)289-5630, 1 (800) 610-1961

- Phillips: (801) 779-7369

- Radio Shack: 1 (800) 442-7221

- Sam's UW: 1 (800) 301-5546, 1 (866) 246-4282

- Sears - Status; 1 (800) 599-9710

- Shell Fleet Card Status Update: 1 (800) 223-3296

- Shell: 1 (800) 223-3296, 1 (866) 438-7435

- Shell: 1 (800) 377-5150

- Staples: Status Line, automated 1-800-767-1275

- Staples: 1(800) 767-1291, 1 (800) 282-5316

- Sunoco Corporate Card: 1(800) 935-3387,(800) 278-6626

- Sunoco: 1 (800) 310-4773

- Target: 1 (800) 440-5317

- Tiffany: 1 (800) 770-0800

- VALERO: 1 (800)324-8464 ACCOUNT STATUS

- Valero: 1 (877) 882-5376

- Wal-Mart: 1(800) 301-5546, underwriting 1 (877) 294-7548
- Wright Express: 1 (888) 743-3893

Hotel Resources

Best Western Corporate
6201 No. 24th Parkway
Pheonix, AZ 85014-2023
1-800-780-7234

Comfort Inn Corporate
10750 Columbia Pike
Silver Spring, MD 209001
1-800-228-5150

Country Inn & Suites By Carlson Corporate
11340 Blondo Street
Omaha, NE 68164
1-888-201-1746

Courtyard By Marriott Corporate
Marriott Drive
Washington DC 20058
1-800-321-2211

Crowe Plaza Corporate
3 Ravinia Drive, Suite 2900
Atlanta, GA 30346
1-800-227-6963

Days Inn Corporate
1918 8th Avenue. NE, Po Box 4090
Aberdeen, SD 57402-4090
1-800-329-7466

Doubletree Corporate
9336 Civic Center Drive
Beverly Hills, CA 90210 1-
800-222-Tree

Embassy Suites Corporate
9336 Civic Center Drive
Beverly Hills, CA 90210 1-
800-362-2779

Fairfield Inn By Marriott Corporate
Marriott Drive
Washington DC 20058
1-800-228-2800

Four Points Corporate
C/O Starwood Hotels& Resorts
1111 Westchester Avenue
White Plains, NY 10604
1-888-625-5144

Four Seasons Corporate
1165 Leslie Street
Toronto, Ontario M3C 2K8
Canada
1-800-819-5053

Hampton Inn & Suites Corporate
9336 Civic Center Drive
Beverly Hills, CA 90210
1-800-426-7866

Hilton Corporate
9336 Civic Center Drive
Beverly Hills, CA 90210
1-800-445-8667

Hilton Garden Inn Corporate
9336 Civic Center Drive
Beverly Hills, CA 90210
1-877-782-9444

Holiday Inn Corporate & Holiday Inn Express 3
Ravinia Drive, Suite 2900
Atlanta, GA 30346-21 49
1-800-465-4329

Homewood Suites By Hilton Corporate
9336 Civic Center Drive
Beverly Hills, CA 90210
1-800-225-4663

Howard Johnson International Corporate
Po Box 27970
Minneapolis, MN 55427-0970
1-800-406-1411

Hyatt Corporate
200 West Madison Street
Chicago, IL 60606
1-800-233-1234

Inter Continental Hotel Group Corporate
3 Ravinia Drive, Suite 2900
Atlanta, GA 30346-21 49
1-877-477-4674

Marriott Hotels& Resorts Corporate
Marriott Drive
Washington DC 20058
1-800-228-9290

Quality Inn Corporate
10750 Columbia Pike
Silver Spring, MD 209001
1-800-424-6423

Radisson Hotels & Resorts Corporate
11340 Blondo Street
Omaha, NE 68164
1-888-201-1718

Renaissance Hotels & Resorts Corporate
Marriott Drive
Washington DC 20058
1-800-468-3571

Residence Inn By Marriott Corporate
Marriott Drive
Washington DC 20058
800-331-3131

Bibliography

Internal Revenue Service
1-800-829-4933 For Businesses
www.irs.gov

Dun and Bradstreet The
D&B Corporation 103
JFK Parkway
Short Hills, NJ 0707
www.dnb.com

Office Suite Plus
(770) 933-6222
www.officesuitesplus.com

Experian
Direct Marketing Services
1-800 588 3657
www.experian.com

HQ Global Workplaces 1
800 956 9543
www.hq.com

National Association of Credit Management
8840 Columbia 100 Parkway
Columbia, Maryland 21045
Telephone: 410/740-5560
Fax: 410/740-5574
http://www.nacm.org/

Business Credit Quick Start

1. Incorporate or Form an LLC

2. Establish a Permanent Business Address

3. Obtain Federal Employer Identification Number (FEIN) (EIN)
www.irs .gov

4. Open a Business Bank Account

5. Business Email address

6. Obtain a D-U-N-S Number

www.dnb.com

7. Comply with Local and State Licensing Laws

Obtain all necessary business licenses, permits, etc.

8. Business Phone

9. Yellow Pages Listing (if you can afford it)

10. Apply for the Creditors Below after steps above have been taken

www.reliable.com

www.nebs.com

www.rapidforms.com

www.uline.com

www.staples.com (make sure you have a phone bill, utility bill or
commercial lease before you apply)